AF587875

BALL IS...

ABCDEFG
HIJKLMN
OPQRSTU
VWXYZ!..

ACORNS

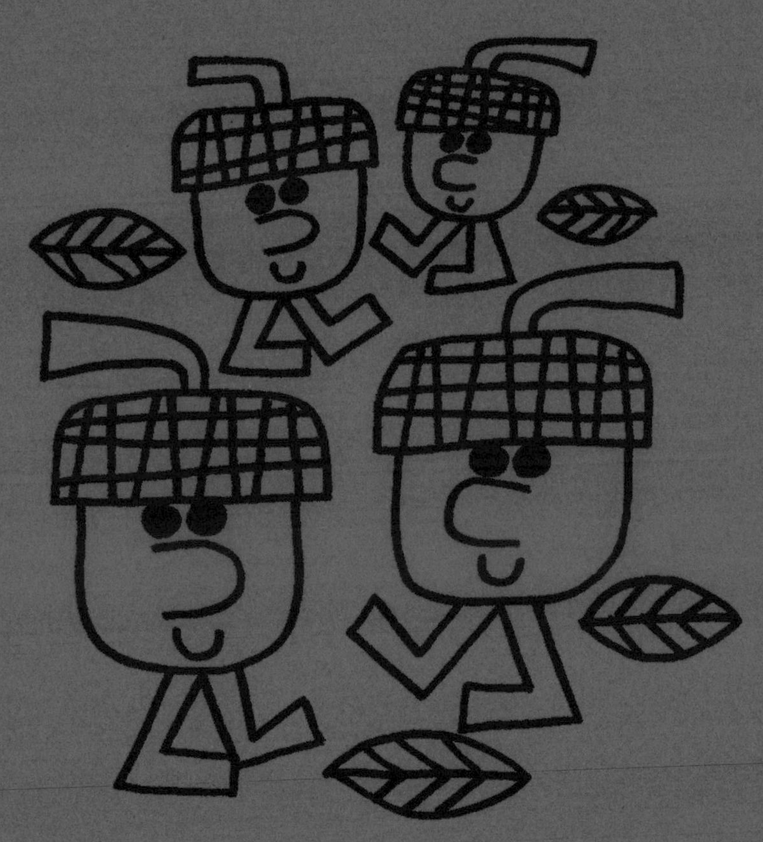

BOO!

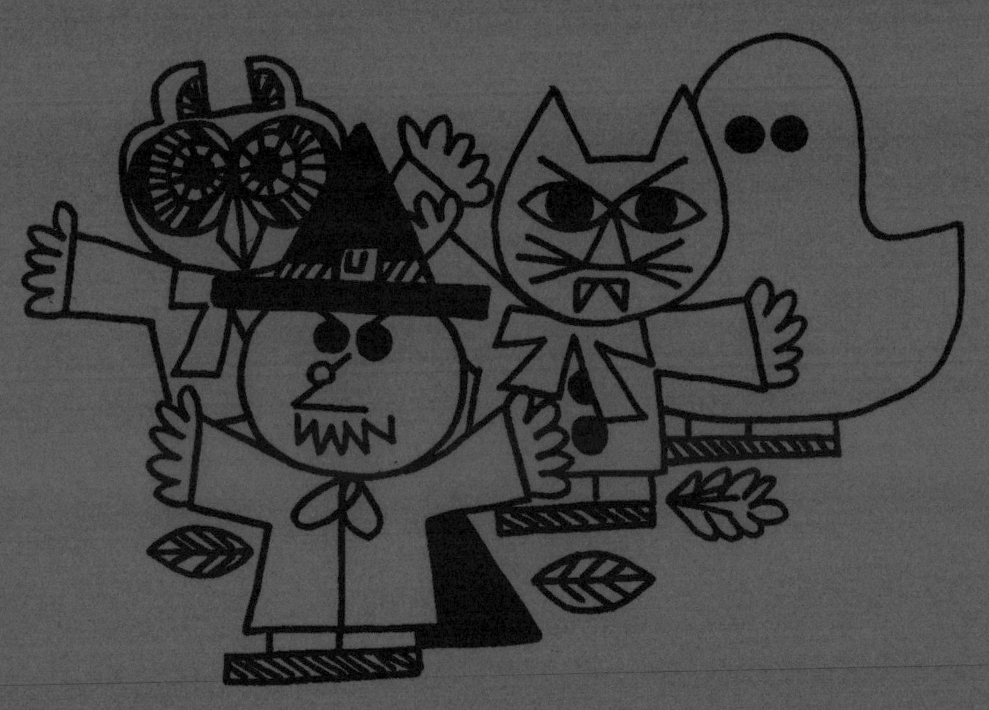

CONDERS

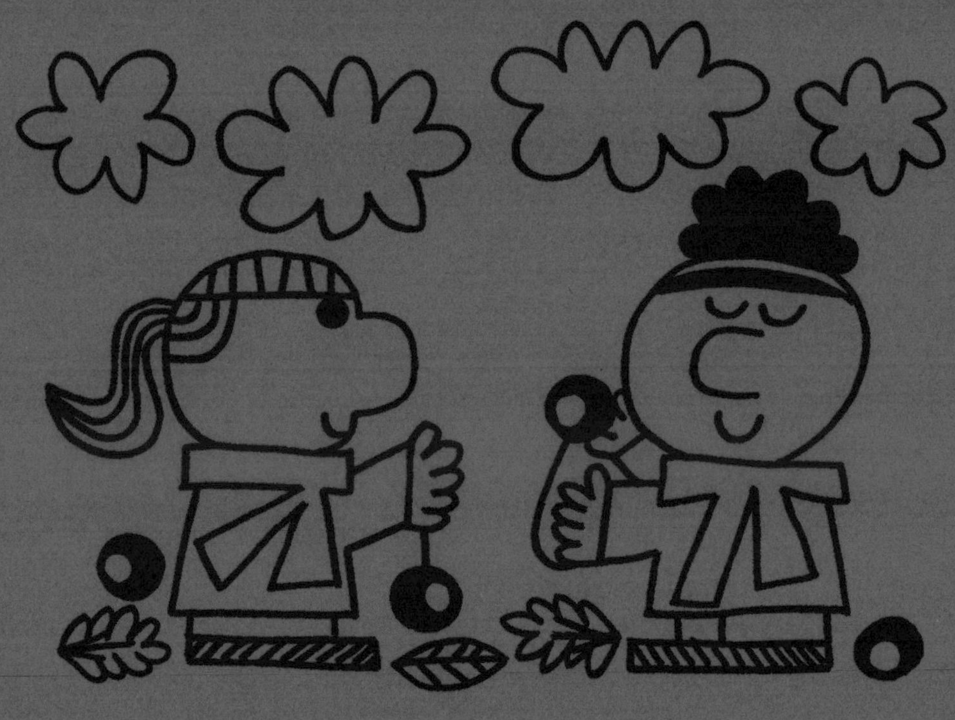

DECIDE

EXPLORE

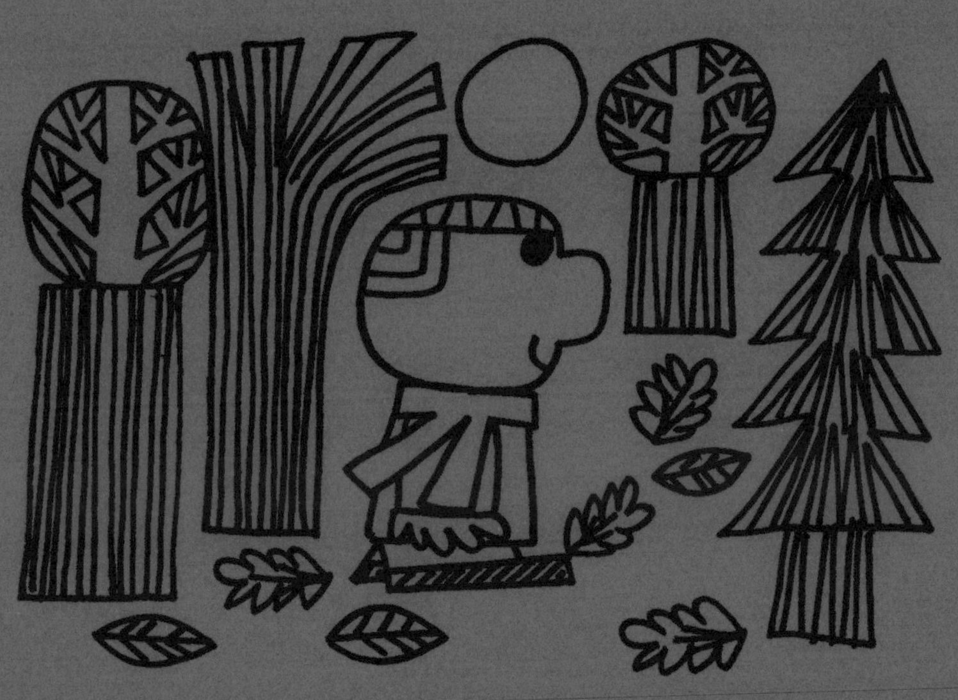

FIRE

GOURD

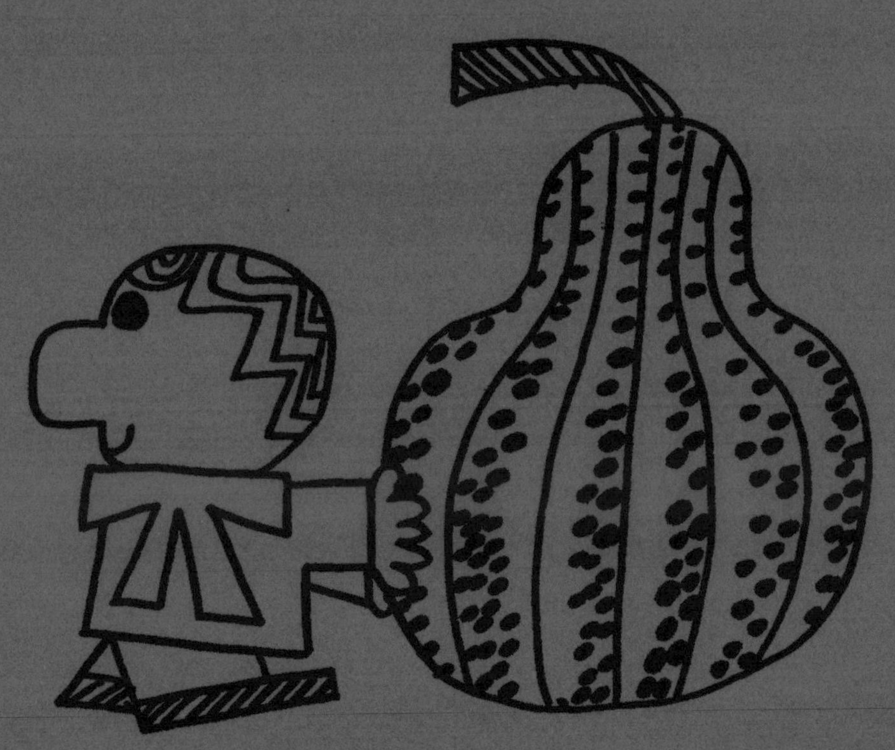

HARVEST

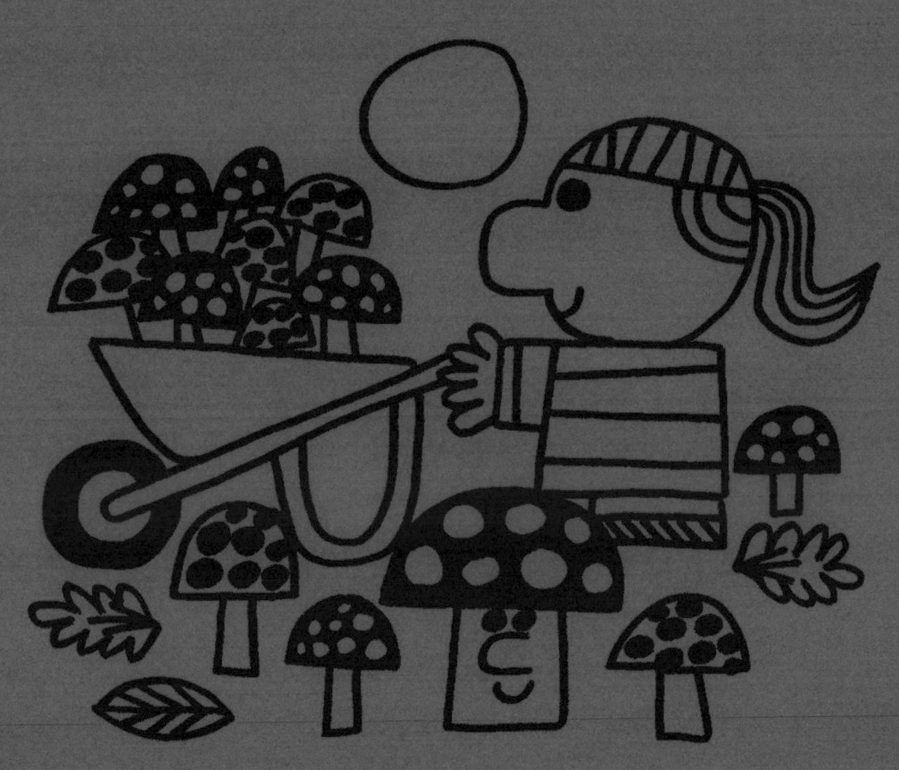

INSECT

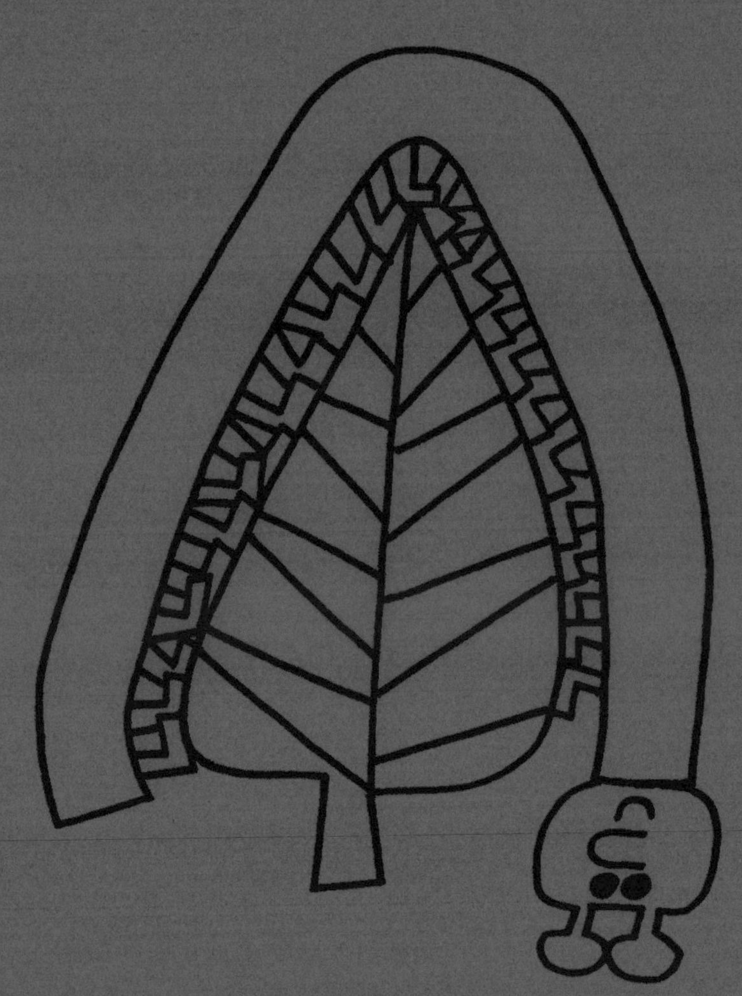

JUMP

BYTE

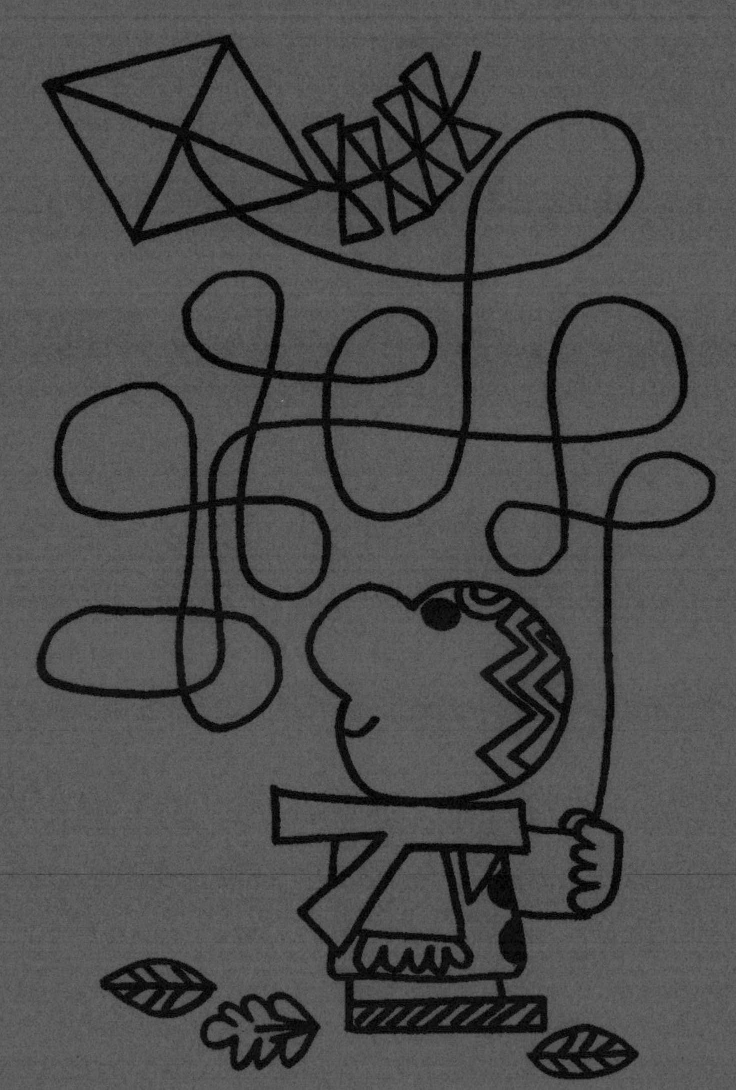

LANTERN

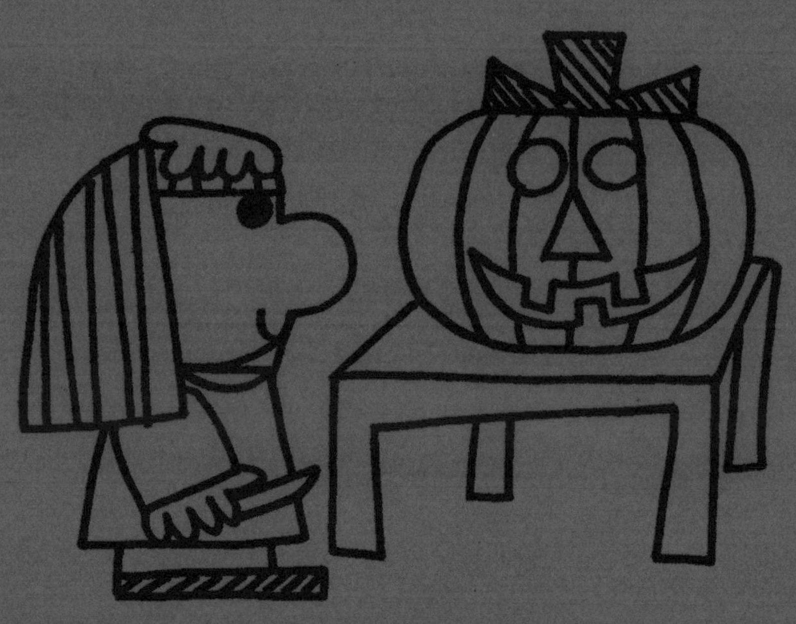

MUSIC

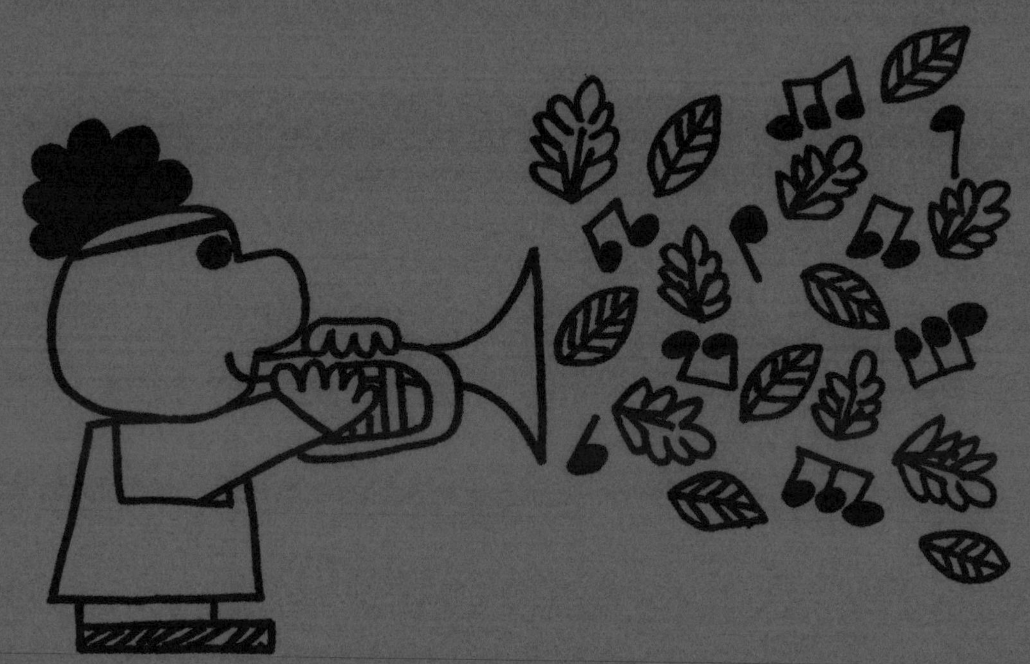

HEAT

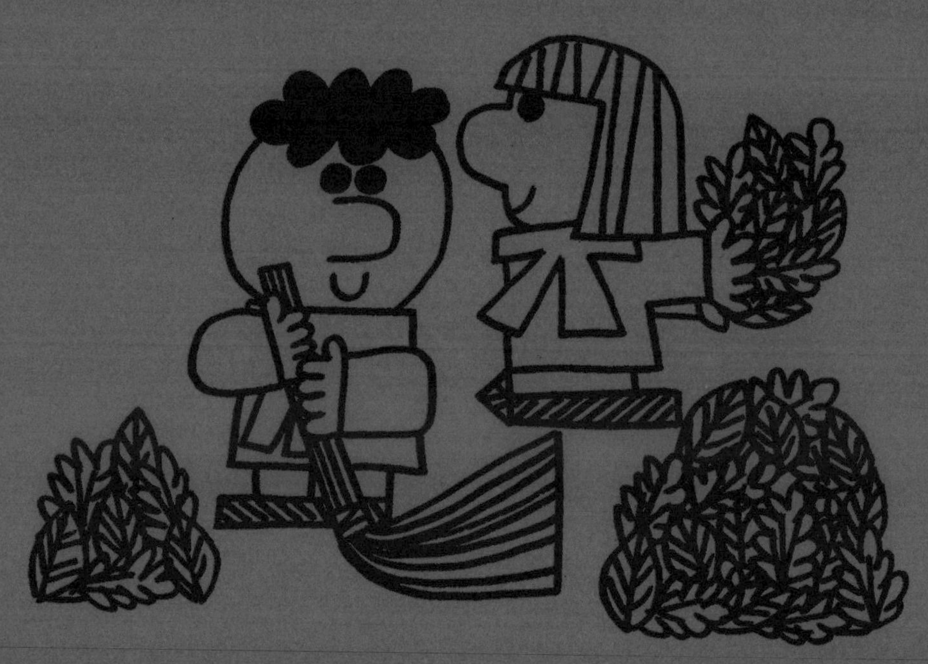

OWL

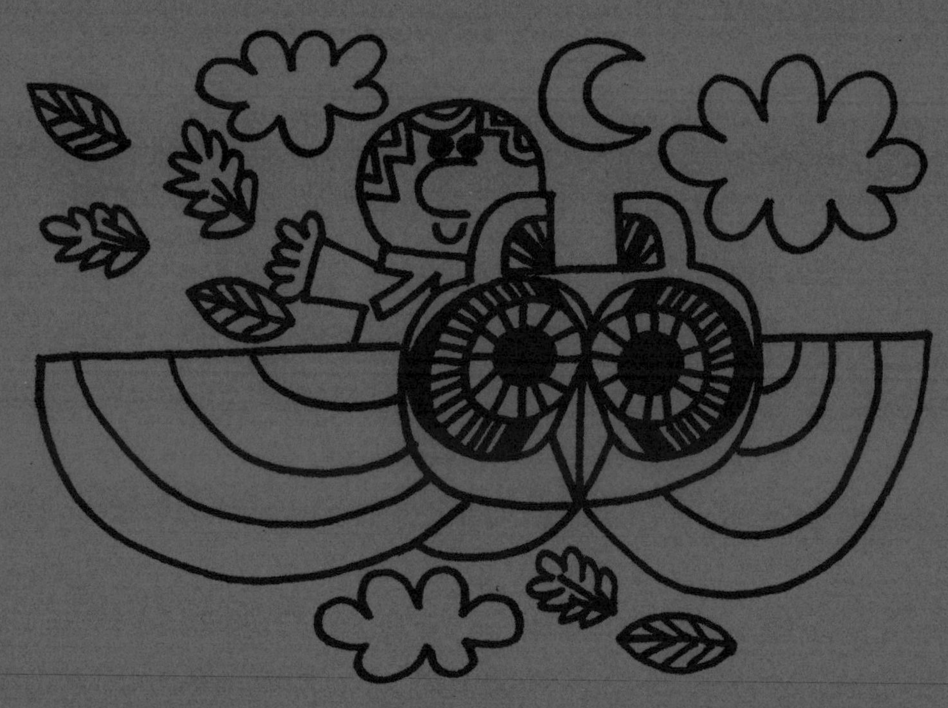

PATTERN

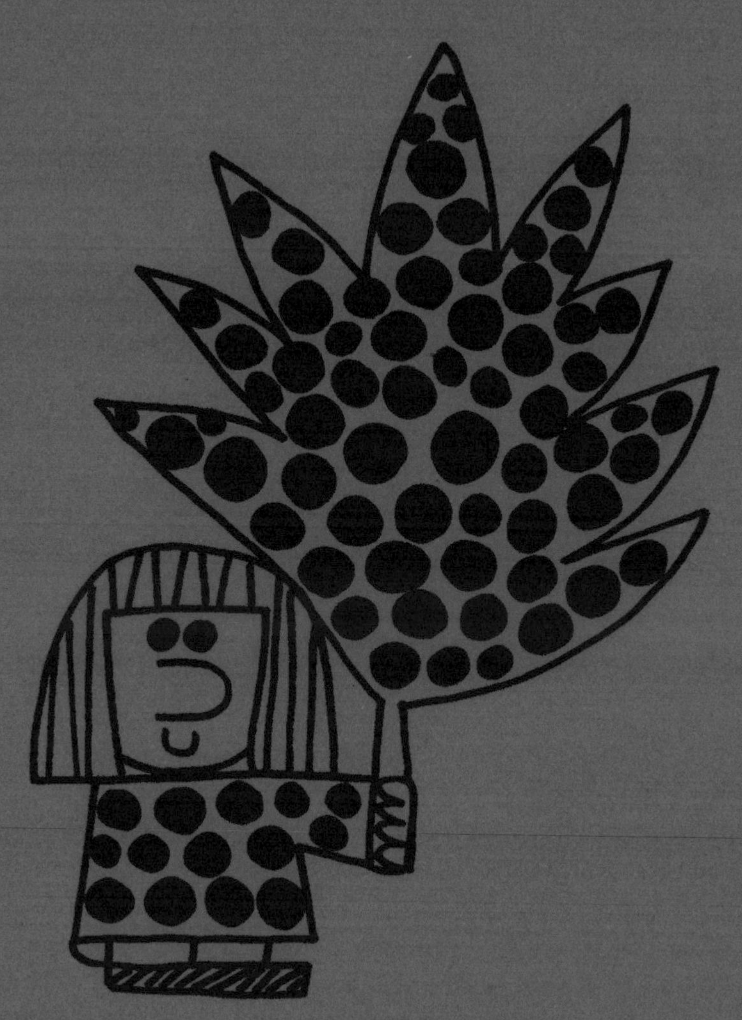

QUILT

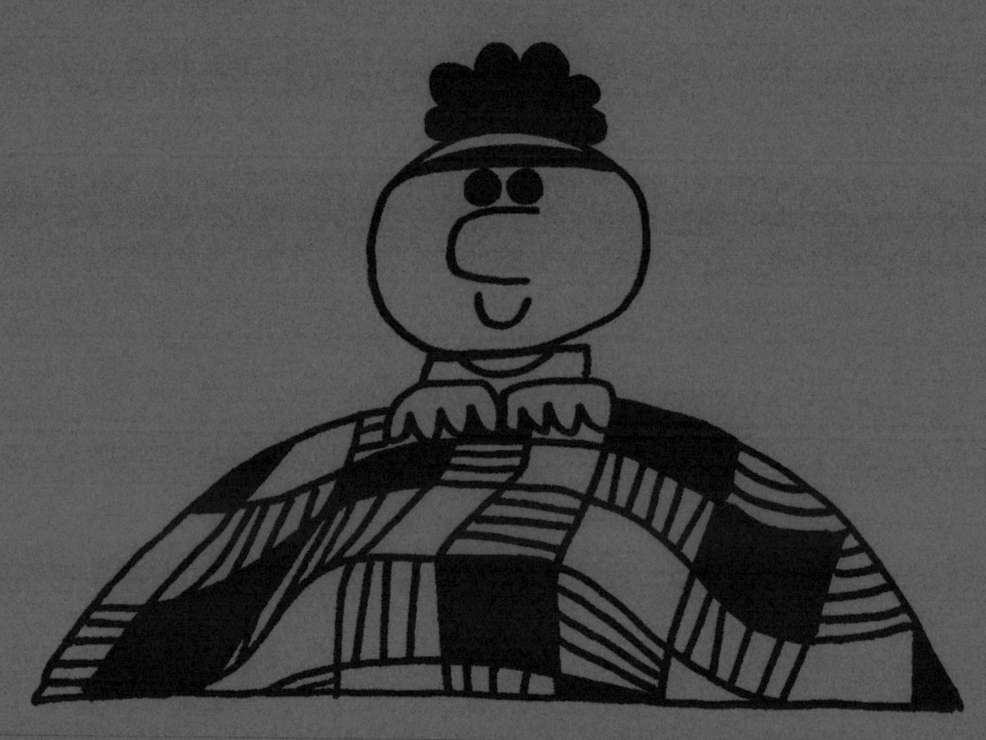

READ

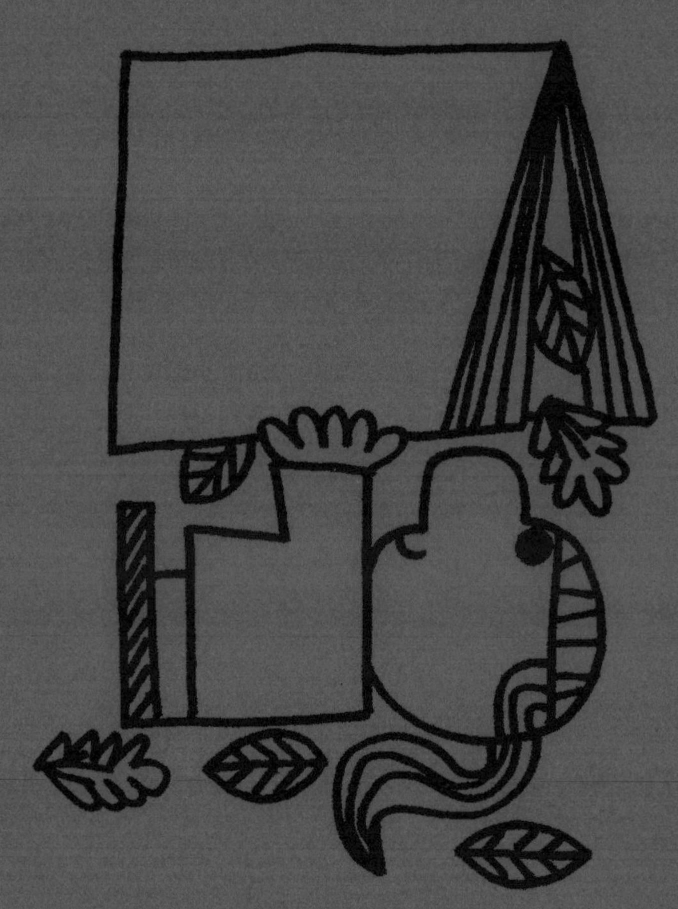

SCHOOL

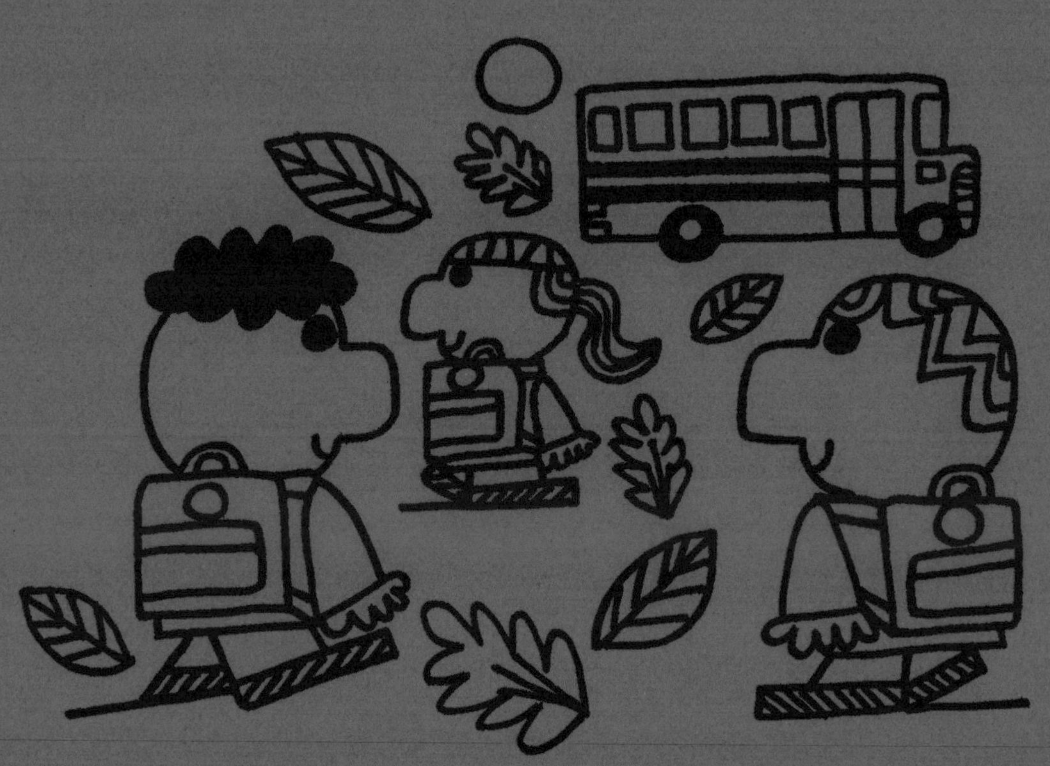

TREE

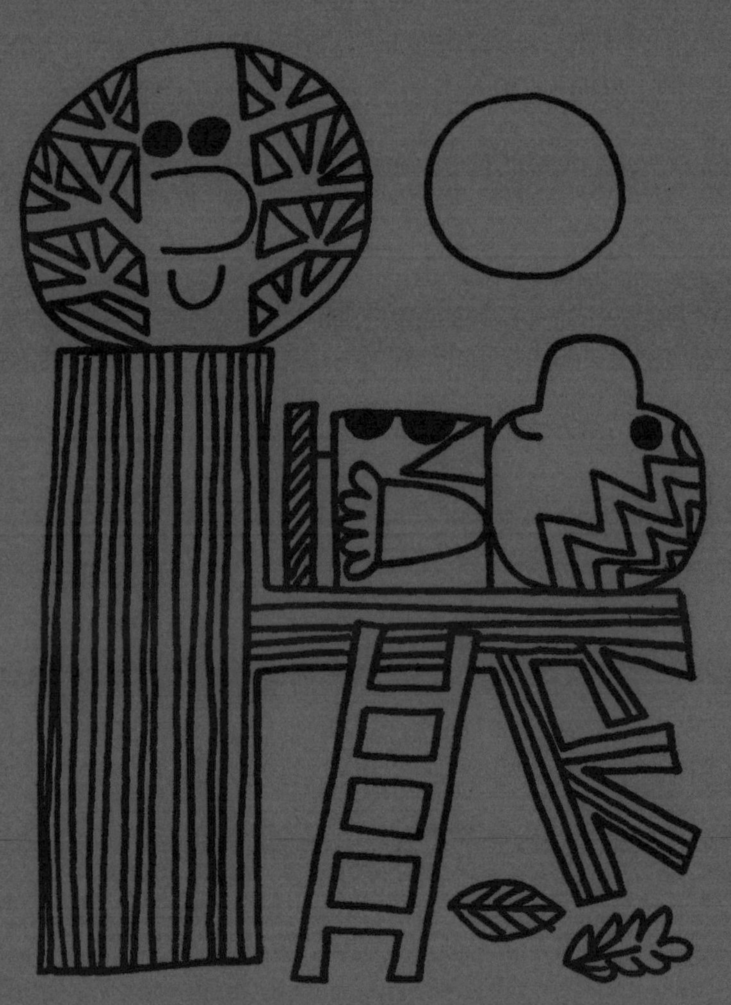

UMBRELLA

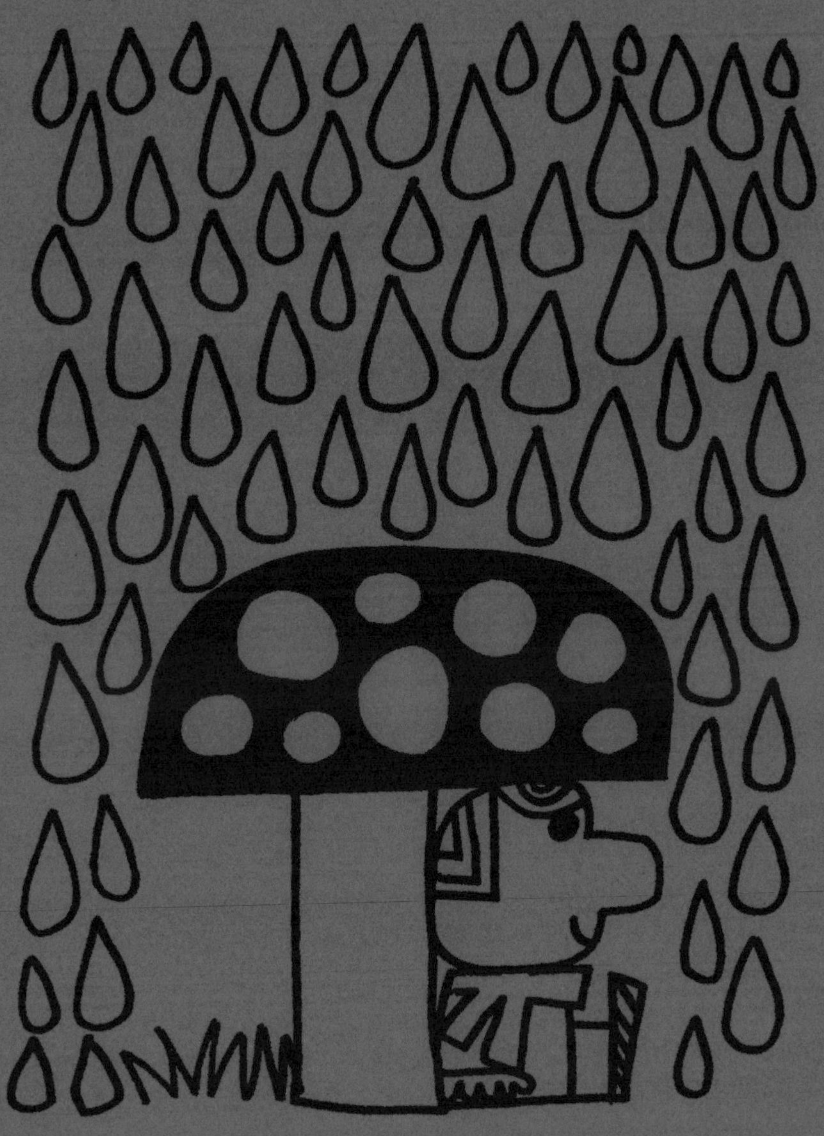

VOYAGE

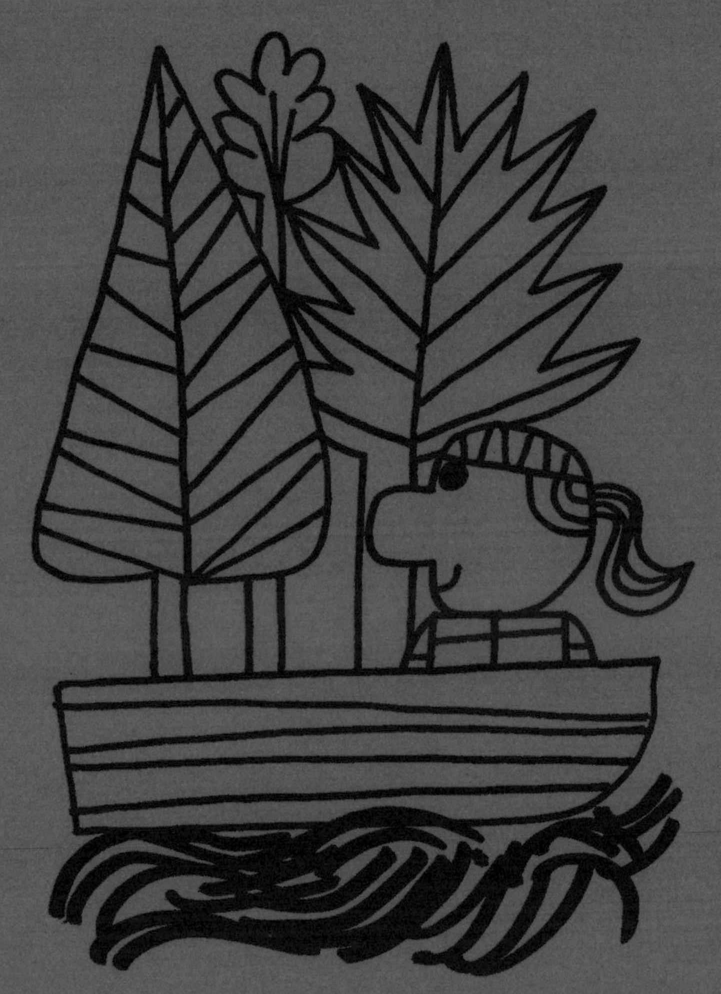

WREATH

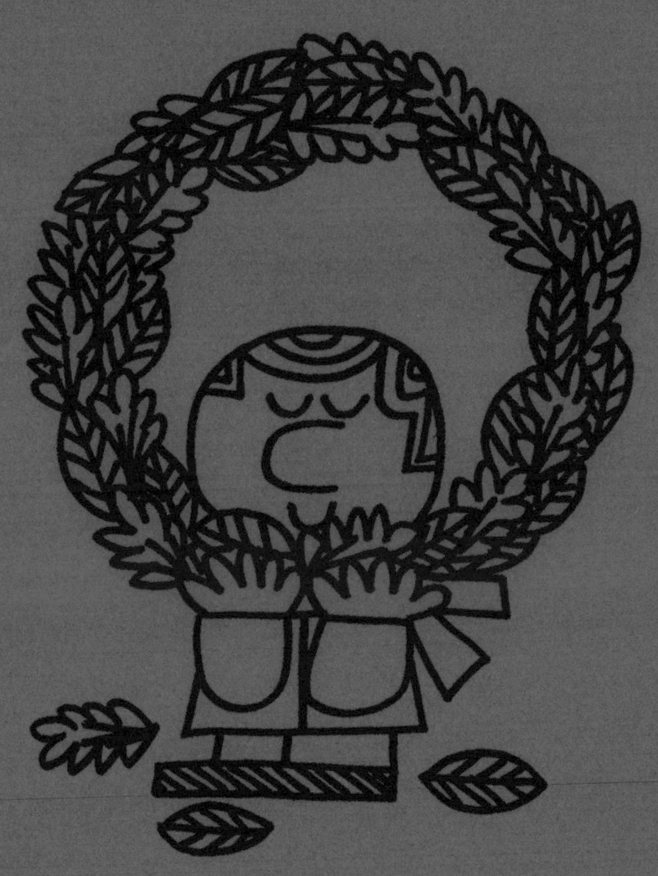

DEROD

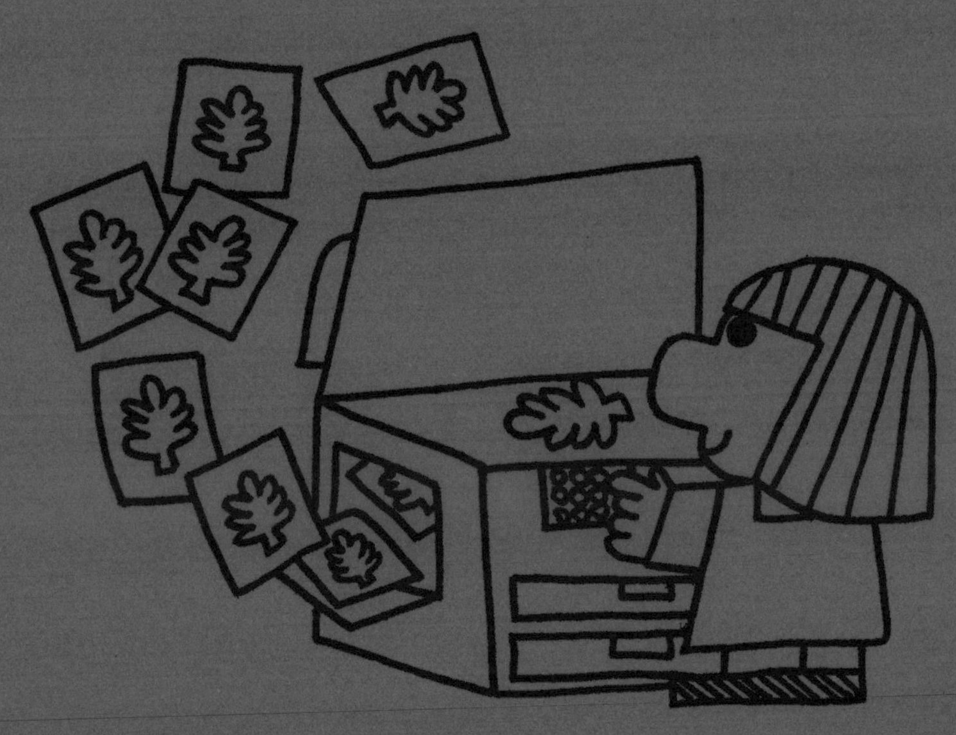

YAWA

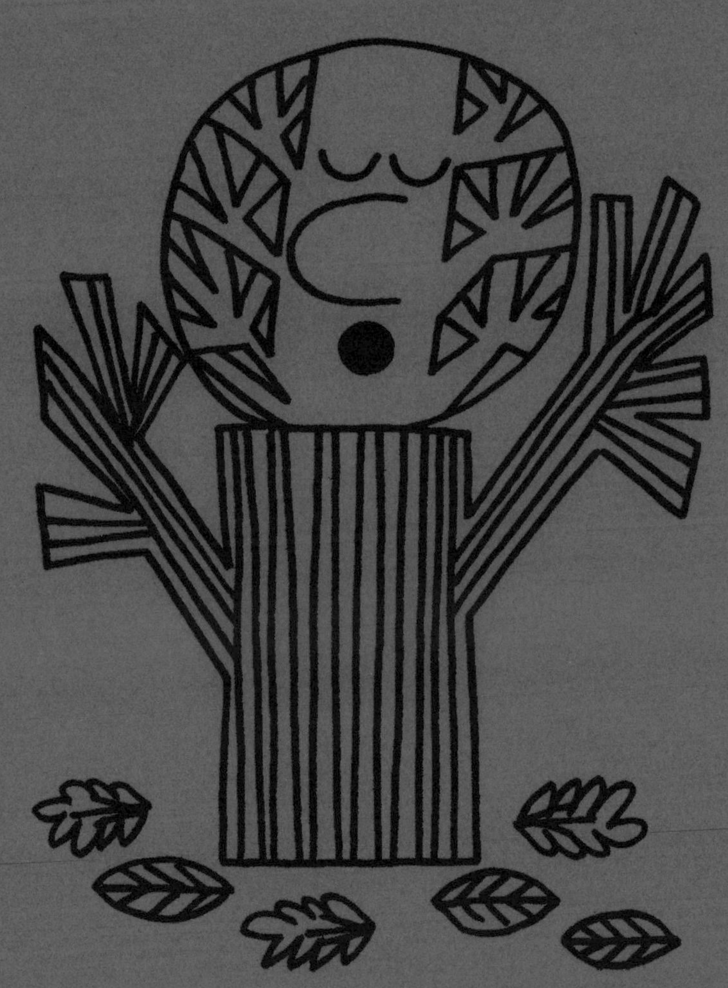

ZOOM!

ADAM HIGTON

ACTUAL
SOURCE
BOOKS

FALL IS...

by ADAM HIGTON
adamhigton.co.uk
@adamhigton

First Edition (Fall 2021)

Published by Actual Source Books
50 E. 500 N. #103
Provo, UT 84606, USA
actualsource.org

ISBN:978-1-7335830-5-3
Catalog# N04-022
Printed in Italy by Conti

Cover: Wibalin Finelinen Black
Pages: Fedrigoni SC Arancio
Ends: Fedrigoni SC Gialloro Rough

Type: All-Fall-Bet (Adam Higton)
Simon Mono (Dinamo)

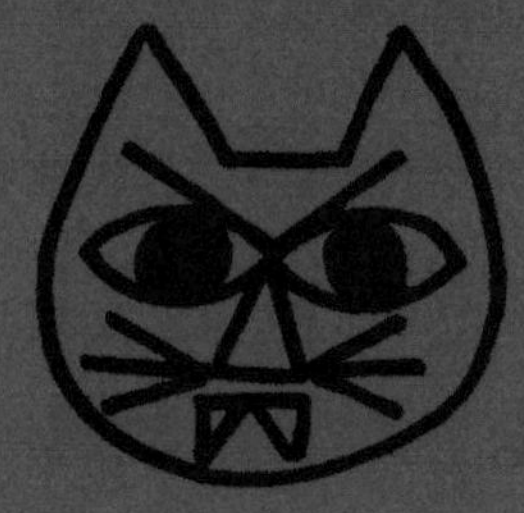